T0068008

Deneen

OUR SPECIAL
BLESSING

BY ANN P. GRANT

WESTBOW
PRESS®
A DIVISION OF THOMAS NELSON
& ZONDERVAN

WestBow Press books may be ordered through
booksellers or by contacting:

WestBow Press
A Division of Thomas Nelson & Zondervan
1663 Liberty Drive
Bloomington, IN 47403
www.westbowpress.com
1 (866) 928-1240

ISBN: 978-1-5127-9832-6 (sc)
ISBN: 978-1-5127-9833-3 (e)

Library of Congress Control Number: 2017912299

Print information available on the last page.

WestBow Press rev. date: 9/25/2017

This book is dedicated to my lovely daughters, Regina, Valencia, and Karla, who endured with me the caring of their sister Deneen. I thank God for each of you, who loved your sister unconditionally. You have always made it known that she was very special to you.

To Deneen, who is in heaven; we all are looking forward to seeing you again.

To my dear son-in-law, Sam, who is really my son; you always encourage me with the words, "Mom, you can do it."

To my grandchildren, Daymein, Brandi, Jason, Brandon, Grant, and Veronica, you exemplified love toward your aunt Deneen that was pleasing to Christ.

To my brother, Dr. Eddie McAnthony, who has always encouraged me to use my God-given talent.

Contents

Acknowledgements

I acknowledge that it is through the goodness of the Lord, my loving Father, that I am blessed with the privilege of writing this book. All of the glory belongs to God for whatever good may come from this book. I recognize and confess that in Him I live, move, and have my being. Therefore, I say to Him, "Thank you, Lord, for choosing me." I could not have done the work on this book without the support of the following people.

Family, you are the best. Through the years as I have taken on projects for the Lord, you've continued your love and loyalty, especially my grandsons, who I would drag with me to all of the churches as I put on my productions. Thank you for being so caring. Your all-around support means so much to me.

Thank God for you, Ann (Annette Jenkins), for being the wonderful Christian woman that you are. Once you read my book, you believed it would be a blessing to all that would read it. You took time from your very busy schedule and went to work helping me to get it published. Your excitement gives me joy. I pray God's goodness in your life always.

To Alice James, my daughter in the Lord, you are so

supportive and I appreciate you. You have participated in so many projects I've done.

I am happy you are an additional daughter and part of our family.

I acknowledge you, my dear friends, Jessie Harris, Dorothy Jenkins, Comel Sherman, Emma Bradley, Martha Bowers, Esther Carter, Dorothy Reece, Mary Reed, and Veida Watson. Thank you for your prayers and support with this project and for so many others through the years.

Thank you, Bessie Love and Sarah Brothers, who took time out from your busy schedules to do my first and second editing.

Endorsements

Reading this book will encourage you to face the many challenges of parenting. The book was written by a very committed, creative, and Spirit-filled person, a mother who embraced her calling to minister to youth and families with special needs children. Her nurturing spirit and godly wisdom have positively influenced the lives of many young men and women.

From the first moment I was introduced to Ann Grant, I could tell that she was chosen to raise her four daughters, viewing them as blessings rather than burdens. It was Thanksgiving of 1980 when I met her and NeeNee while attending one of our many holiday celebrations. I witnessed their loving interaction as NeeNee would circle the house searching the house for her mother just to lay her head on her mother's shoulders. There was a special bond between them that continued throughout NeeNee's life. As you read and share in their experiences, you will undoubtedly examine your own times of struggles, trials, tears, joy, laughter, and smiles, realizing that God gives strength and grace to fulfill your call to care.

—Pastor Steaven M. Hawkins

God has inspired Ann to write this wonderful book about her challenging experiences in the growth and development of her special needs daughter. Ann's walk with God has been strengthened through the life she and her daughter shared. I am sure that all who read this book will be greatly blessed.

—Jessie D. Harris

This book is written to show the world how God blesses families who have special needs children. It is about the life of a special needs person who was a part of a family that loved her dearly. This book shows how God loves and blesses each person. This book will be a blessing to all who read it. Ann's story is a constant reminder that we are all fearfully and wonderfully made. To God be the glory.

—Martha C. Bowers

Little NeeNee was so precious. She could not speak, but she could communicate. I remember on one occasion the congregation was meeting in the social hall of the church. NeeNee came to me and led me to the piano in the sanctuary. She remembered I was the pianist. I played and gave NeeNee her own private concert. She loved music. It makes me happy to know that she is now in the presence of angels, listening to heavenly music. As you read this book, you will be encouraged and strengthened by the love, patience, and care shown for little NeeNee by her mother and family.

—Veida Watson

Introduction

I wrote this book about my daughter because I have come to know that God chooses to use people to do the work He knows they are capable of doing. All experiences we have in life can always be a blessing to someone if we are willing to share with others how God brought us through. I pray that it will be a book of encouragement to parents of special needs children, whether they are mentally challenged or have been diagnosed with Down syndrome, autism, cerebral palsy, childhood cancer, sickle cell anemia, or any other birth defects or health issues with which parents in these situations must deal. I also pray that this book will encourage those who suddenly find themselves placed in the position of caregiver to their loved ones—a position that, although you did not choose it, you have determined to do your very best because God has chosen, called, and assigned you to the task.

As God gives each of us a task, He also gives us the strength to carry it out.

If we trust Him, it will not always be easy, but it can be done. There are ups and downs we must face, but through it all, we will find a life filled with rewards. There is no way I could put everything about the forty-four years of life with my special blessing in this one book; therefore, this book was written as a day of reflection, as I began my day with the Lord, studying the Bible and reading my devotional. I reflected on events that allowed me to share the truths of God's word that sustained me through various challenges and struggles throughout the years of caring for my special needs daughter. Focusing on the truths of God's word that I share, in my time of reflection, is where comfort, support, and encouragement will be found. This same comfort, support, and encouragement is available to all who are in need and especially for those who share a similar task of providing care for a loved one who has special needs.

Remember that all of God's promises are yes and amen. I know that His promises are real from experience. God will not leave nor forsake you (Hebrews 13:5). May God bless you as you read *Deneen: Our Special Blessing.*

Prologue

God Created Special People
Dedicated to Deneen, my special daughter

God created special people to help make us smile,
and He said, "Enjoy them now, it's only for a while."

Special people were created with a special touch.
They love unconditionally, and it means so very much.

God created special people to do the Master's will.

They live the life that's given them, His word to fulfill.

Special people were created, even though
there's so much they cannot do.

But they never stop trying, and the
Lord sees them through.

God created special people, although
many folk don't understand.

To them they are different, but
part of God's perfect plan.

God created special people to teach
us unconditional love
and to let us know that they are
special gifts sent from above.

Special people were created to show the world the way,
to live a life filled with happiness, with God every day.

Ann P. Grant Jan. 16, 2003

Joy and Sadness

There isn't anything special about today. The sun is shining bright. It's a bit warm, but it's an ordinary September morning. I am sitting at the dining room table having coffee and reading my Bible and daily devotionals. As usual, I am starting my day with the Lord. My plan is to make a peach cobbler and a couple of lemon pies, but this morning I find myself lost in my thoughts of NeeNee, who was *my* special blessing. She should be standing at the window looking at things going on outside, one of her favorite things to do. However, I reflect on the past years of my life and just how far I have traveled on my journey. I reminisce about events that brought me to this present time. With every thought, I can see now that the Lord was working in my life for the good. But all of the events in my life were *not* good. There was a failed marriage, many financial struggles, sickness, and raising four daughters alone. In retrospect, trusting in His will, I can see that indeed God's goodness has worked in my life many times over.

Any day is better when we start it with the Lord.

This is the day the Lord has made; we
will rejoice and be glad in it.

(Psalm 118:24)

On January 14, 2009, my whole world changed. My youngest daughter, Deneen, my special blessing, left me to be with the Lord. As I sit here thinking about how events occurred, Deneen is still very much alive in my heart. Looking back, I shared an unforgettable life with Deneen and her sisters. It's a funny thing about memories. They do not appear in chronological order, and the laughter and the sadness sometimes intersperse. I know I must continue. As I go about my daily activities, there is a painful void, and that void can only be filled when I feel the peace and comfort of my loving heavenly Father.

As I sit here, I can still see all my little girls. The oldest one, Regina, was always the little mother. The second one, Valencia, was five years older than her little sister, but she wanted to remain the baby. The third one, Karla, always had a quick answer. The very special baby, Deneen (fondly called NeeNee and who we all loved to no end), was my fourth. My daughters are the very best! I remember the tough times we went through and the help my daughters were to me. Being self-employed had its ups and downs, but my sustaining power was the Lord. I found happiness in my girls and in my love for the Lord and His work. As I sit here sipping coffee, I think about the years of working in the barbershop to support my daughters. It was a necessary convenience since I was a single parent. Many times I had to leave work early or stay home. In some ways, it was the best thing, since I was alone raising my children—but never *really* alone. I thank God for where I am today.

We should know that we are never alone,
because God is always with us.

For God Himself has said "I will never leave you
Nor forsake you." (Hebrews 13:5 NKJV)

2

My Baby

My baby was born on October 8, 1964. She was a perfect doll—so lovable and cuddly with her black curly hair. I named her Deneen Elizabeth, Elizabeth being my mother's name. Deneen would be my last child, and I loved that precious baby girl. When my baby girl was born, I made the statement, "This is *my* baby." How prophetic, for indeed my baby would always remain mentally a baby of nearly a year old.

I remember the love and joy I had when I saw my baby, but a short three months later, my joy turned into pain. I began to realize that my baby was different. I started praying and seeking the Lord about NeeNee, but I really knew in my heart that my precious baby was not developing as she should. She could not hold up her head, nor could she turn over. When she cried, you could barely hear her, and she paid no attention to anything around her. I knew that was not normal.

Everyone tried to tell me that it was new-baby nervousness, but I never accepted that. In my heart, I knew something was wrong. Even my doctor did not believe me, but I knew. After many tests and examinations, I finally received the diagnosis that Deneen was severely mentally disabled. She was also diagnosed with cerebral palsy, and her life expectancy was not expected to exceed twenty-one years. Deneen defied the odds. Not only did she live twenty-one years, but she lived forty-four years. The morning sun is entering my dining room in all its glory, and I remember the pain I felt upon hearing the devastating news of her medical condition.

Every mother wants a perfectly normal child. Now the full implications of my words came back to me—indeed she is my baby, and did I ever pray.

Prayer was the key to my staying power. I leaned on the Lord, knowing that there is nothing impossible for God. Today I still lean on Him, knowing that His keeping power has sustained me to this present time in my life. The Lord gives us an invitation to call Him, and He will always answer. This promise has always been comforting to me.

While I continue to let the thoughts of my loss flow through my mind, I'm crying from the pain. But when I think about NeeNee, I can also laugh; she would do so many things that would seriously make me chuckle. That also is the goodness of the Lord. I thought of the words the doctor told me about my baby.

He said, "Please don't put her in an institution. She will not do as well as she will do at home with her family who loves her."

I remember saying to the doctor, "That thought never

crossed my mind. This is my baby, and she is part of our family; we will love her and will not be ashamed of her."

I was speaking, of course, of the children and me. We did not live as a family with a secret in the closet. Deneen was very much an active member of our family. I did not realize how many special needs children are in foster care until I was blessed with one. I thank God with all my heart that I was able to keep Deneen home. I can still see some of the events that happened during her life, now realizing that God had it all planned out.

It is Saturday, and I have no particular plans. I just want to sit and consider the goodness of the Lord. I was going to make a peach cobbler and some lemon pies, but for now I just want to enjoy the precious memories of NeeNee.

The Lord's invitation to call Him
has always been comforting.

Call to Me, and I will answer you, and show
you great and mighty things, which you
do not know. (Jeremiah 33:3 NKJV)

3

Love Shown

As I look again out of the window, I think to myself, *This is September 26, exactly two months and twenty-four days until Christmas. What a change in my life now.* I remember with thanksgiving that first Christmas I had alone with my girls after my divorce. I remember how my friends got together over forty years ago to see to it that my daughters had a very perfect Christmas. My husband left us exactly one week before Christmas on December 18, 1965, and he left us with only twenty dollars and no means to give my children a merry Christmas. I remember how my friends used redemption stamps, along with their personal financial contributions, to help make our Christmas merry. I smile today thinking about those redemption stamps. They were trading stamps, and they were very popular during the sixties and seventies. They were given at supermarkets, gas stations, and other participating stores. After filling the booklets, they were redeemable for small appliances, clothes, tools, toys, and jewelry.

I can never forget the happiness of my daughters that Christmas morning! I find myself still thanking God again for His faithfulness then as well as now for the love of family and friends. During that time, God delivered me from false pride. That life experience taught me there would be times in my life when I would face situations of need, and the blessings from God would be through fellowship of others. I realized that when there is a need in my life, there is no reason to be ashamed to ask for help. Being prideful will never meet our needs.

Speaking of Christmas, NeeNee loved to unplug the Christmas tree lights. We would decorate for Christmas with all kinds of lights in the living room, but when we would walk into the room, we would find it dark. It would be a nightly battle trying to keep those lights on. We always had to find a way to stop her antics, so we plugged the lights into another socket that she couldn't reach. One time we had singing angels on the tree, and the music was rather loud. NeeNee unplugged them and did not allow the angels to sing—poor angels. If the Christmas decoration was small and she liked it, it always ended up on the sofa. The family learned to accept her ways. We knew in her own way, she loved Christmas.

I think about Christmas of 1974—the trip we made with my sister and her family in their RV to Dallas, Texas, to visit my mother. The long journey really unnerved NeeNee. She didn't like being out of her usual surroundings, but as a family, we worked together to make the best of it. My mother was a great cake baker, and when we arrived, there were all kinds of delicious cakes on the hutch in the dining room. Sometime during the day, my mother noticed that someone had grabbed a chunk of the chocolate cake with his or her hands and eaten it. My mother was quite upset until we went into the den and saw NeeNee with chocolate all over her face and hands. Needless to say, in her own way NeeNee said to me that day, "I like chocolate." From then on, I started to feed her chocolate pudding.

NeeNee didn't necessarily like cake, but she did like chocolate. I used chocolate pudding because it was easier for her to swallow. I thank God; it was His leading that allowed me to notice different things to do for her to make life as happy as I could. People with little or no speech still have the same communication needs as the rest of us. You may just have to work a bit harder to find a communication strategy that works. They relate in their own ways, as demonstrated in the case of the chocolate cake. No one can take credit, for it is God's wisdom that leads us, and when we rely on His wisdom, the lines of communication will remain open.

I had a part-time job before I reentered barbering college. Things had begun to look a little better because of the extra income. Then I received the news that I could return to barbering college to become licensed and able to work as a barber. I was very happy, and I truly recognized that God was faithful, and He had not forgotten my need to have a reliable source of income. I had to be at work at 7:00 a.m. I had to get the children ready and leave them to go to school. It is always painful to leave your children alone. We didn't have a car and many times the weather was bad, but we persevered. The girls helped by taking NeeNee to the sitter before they went to school. I went to work and afterward had to take a bus across town to barbering school. We continued this routine until the Lord blessed me with a car through our pastor. The car was a relief to our family, but I have not nor will I ever forget the kindness of my friends.

I wasn't the first single parent to struggle with children, and I won't be the last. I made it because the Lord was the strength of my life, and He still is.

We must remember at all times God can do anything. Nothing is impossible with Him.

Behold, I am the Lord, the God of all flesh. Is there anything too hard for Me? (Jeremiah 32:27 NKJV)

I regret the responsibility that my daughters had to share, but I thank God that I still have their love and respect. The love of family is unending, and my daughters are the best. I am happy because they loved their baby sister and also love each other.

NeeNee took the bottle until the age of six. Her first school was at a rehabilitation hospital in Southern California. When I think about that time, my heart always gets heavy because I had to trust my baby to strangers. I was afraid they would mistreat her. When they told me to not send her bottle or to give it to her at home anymore, I thought that was so cruel. Now as I look back, I know just how wrong I was. I saw these people showing so much love and determination toward my daughter. They would crawl around on the floor, working with my child and others like her trying to get them to do even the smallest thing—like being able to hold up their heads. They taught me that there was always hope.

The instructors were trying to teach NeeNee to eat solid food because she never learned to chew and had a hard time swallowing. She had an abnormally small swallowing passage. All of her life I had to puree her food. I remember the time I decided to teach her to feed herself. I put a spoon in her hand and watched as she attempted to eat. After cleaning food from the ceiling, wall, and floor, I realized that she could not feed herself. However, she did progress, but she was still classified as unteachable. Those were the painful times.

Deneen did not walk until she was six years old. But God gave us the strength to carry her. She attended three developmental centers at elementary schools during her early years of life. I found mentally challenged people to be very trusting and very loving. That's when I became aware that I was her protector. She depended on me since she could not speak. I had to be watchful. God blessed our family to watch over her at all times, and I thank God that His angels truly watched over her and us during the time she was with us.

The greatest gift of all is love, and
family love is unending.

Love suffers long and is kind; love does
not envy; love does not parade itself, is
not puffed up. (1 Corinthians 13:4)

New Beginning

NeeNee attended several schools for special needs children. After reaching the age of twenty-one and being classified as an adult, the law required that she graduate from the elementary school campus in Downy, California and be moved to an adult facility. The graduation ceremony was beautiful, and although it meant nothing to NeeNee, it meant everything to me. Consider if you will a twenty-one-year-old adult with the actions of an eighteen-month baby. But I had no choice but to find an adult program for her. That meant I had new worries. I enrolled her in a facility for mentally challenged adult citizens, where she attended for twenty-three years. It was a special place that showed so much love and concern for all of their clients. They called her Miss Grant sometimes because of the way she acted. She always acted as if she knew that she was special to us. Sometimes the workers would call me at home and ask what fragrance she was wearing that day. I always made sure that she would look and smell pretty. It makes me smile and even laugh when I think about NeeNee's vanity.

The staff at facility were wonderful people. The love they had for the clients placed the parents at ease. When I was interviewed to place NeeNee there, I started crying because I was afraid to leave her with these strangers. Many years later the director told me that, when I cried, she was almost afraid to accept NeeNee into the program because of my response. She thought I was going to be one of those fanatical mothers, but with God's help, I learned to trust them and we forged a wonderful bond. Anxieties were unnecessary when I saw how NeeNee enjoyed being there. She loved being with her special friends and did not want to miss any days at the center. She was very happy when she was there. When I visited her center, she would react as if I was not a part of her life there. I would tell her, "I am leaving. I will see you at home." But if I was picking her up, she would leave with me and be happy. My friend and neighbor, Doris, cared for her in the afternoon after she came home from the center until I got home from work. When I would get home from work and walk over to get NeeNee, sometimes she pretended that she was not going to leave with me, so after visiting for a while, I would say to NeeNee, "Come on, missy, let's go home." She would pretend she didn't hear me. Then I would say, "Okay, I'm going to leave," and she would ignore me until I started out of the door. Then she would move in her kind of rush and grab my hand. Those were the cute things that I miss. That was her way of having fun with her mommy. I was so blessed to have a family of neighbors who also loved my daughter. Doris cared for NeeNee until she had a stroke and was unable to perform the task.

The year NeeNee turned twenty-one was a great celebration with family and friends. Over one hundred people were in attendance at her birthday party. You might wonder what she thought about all of those people at her house celebrating her life. The truth is absolutely nothing! The party took place in our backyard, and she stayed outside about twenty minutes. Then she went back inside the house and looked out the door for the remainder of the celebration. All those people represented change, and she tensed up when things were different. I was able to get her to stay outside for our pastor, Rev. Walter Washington, to pray for her. We had to celebrate what God had done in NeeNee's life, which proved that God holds our being in His hands and that He is in control.

NeeNee reaching the age of twenty-one came with some additional concerns. NeeNee needed extra protection because she was constantly progressing. We needed to watch her more closely. She had now learned how to use the light switch, and she turned the lights on and off at the wrong times. She discovered the water faucet and often flooded the kitchen and bathroom. She learned how to go outside, and I found her crossing the street to my friend Doris's house. God was faithful, and He truly protected her and us.

NeeNee even deceived Doris. Doris had stairs in her home. NeeNee was afraid of the stairs, or so we all thought. Somehow she would go up the stairs without anyone seeing her. Doris would bring her down on her back because she thought she didn't know how to get downstairs. Then one of Doris's daughters caught her coming down and said to her, "You are busted!" After that Doris told her the next time she went up those stairs, she would bring herself down. Sure enough, NeeNee came down those stairs over and over again. God proved again that His protection was all around her. After we discovered that she had learned to do something, she would always give us her smile when we would praise her for a new accomplishment. This little person had so many ways of communicating through her actions. I had finally learned that worrying was not the answer.

I learned then and know it to be true even
now that worrying is not the answer.

Be anxious for nothing, but in everything by
prayer and supplication, with thanksgiving,
let your requests be made known to God.
(Philippians 4:6 NKJ)

The Task

Having a combined living and dining room, I can always see the sofa where my daughter kept all of the things she enjoyed. Imagine, if you will, stuffed animals, jewelry, spoons, cooking utensils, purses, brushes, combs, cologne, box cake mix, canned soda, books, keys, and toys. Anything that appealed to her belonged to her. The family named it NeeNee's stash. I remember how I prayed for God to heal my baby. I asked my friends to attend healing services with me. I called healing prayer lines. I sent money to healers. I found it hard to believe that God couldn't turn things around. He could, but He didn't. As I grew closer to the Lord through the study of His word and started listening to God and not to the things that man said, I noticed a change in my life. I accepted what God had for me to do. I finally accepted the fact that God had given me a child with special needs who turned into a special blessing. And with this blessing, He had a special task for me to do. He assured me that I would not be alone.

Then I decided to get busy in the service of the Lord by being a mother to a special needs child.

In the midst of raising my other daughters, I thought about all of the unpleasant things that came along with being the mother of a special needs child. There was the drooling, the diapers, and the funny way she walked. Sometime she would also walk on her knees, which a lot of people found hard to understand. I taught my girls to wipe her mouth and keep her face clean, change her diapers, feed her, and entertain her. Her look changed as she got older. She could not keep her mouth closed, and there was drooling. I remember the pain I felt in my heart when I allowed the doctors to perform surgery on her saliva glands to stop the drooling. That was a big mistake. That's when I made the decision to never do anything to cause her unnecessary pain. I could not forget the pain and the look in NeeNee's eyes. I cried every day until I brought her home. I looked into her eyes and realized I had caused her unnecessary pain for something she had no control over. With that I decided that wiping her mouth was not so hard to do. I tried using a bib to help, but she would pull them off. The family just worked hard to keep her face clean.

No mother expects to be changing diapers for forty-four years, nor to still be feeding a child either, but after a while, it became a natural thing to do. I thought about all of the stares from people who just didn't know any better. I shed a lot of tears, but I didn't give up. There were many trips to the hospital dealing with doctors who did not understand how to treat a patient who could not explain her problem. I had to speak on NeeNee's behalf. After her sisters became adults, they were definitely her advocates. We were all that NeeNee had to stand on her behalf. I remember the time that she had trouble walking, and she couldn't tell me where she was hurting. That's when I felt her pain and when my pain was greatest. She could not speak, yet I knew she was hurting. I remember taking her to the emergency room, on one of many trips. They didn't find the cause, but I insisted that something was wrong. I moved NeeNee's toe, and she reacted with pain. I pointed it out to the doctor. He then had her foot x-rayed and found that she had a fractured toe.

It was always painful to see her suffer. It was really hard for our family to endure. I often wondered if she thought that pain and suffering were the norm for her. She could not speak, and I think she just quietly surrendered to the pain. During her pain, I wondered sometimes if NeeNee thought I didn't love her. Out of forty-four years, there were many sick days, and I suffered with her, but I found consolation in knowing that God knew and He cared. He saw us through every sickness until the final sickness came. Don't think that I didn't have many pity parties. I shed lots and lots of tears, but through those years I was blessed to have Christian friends who would not let me party too long. I have one friend in particular who would always say, "I'm not attending your party!" We would always have a good laugh. Thank God for friends who always reminded me of the goodness of the Lord.

My daughter Valencia moved back home with us in 2001. That was the year I retired from barbering after thirty-five years. Valencia was a great help to me with her sister. After having problems with her heart, she could no longer work. Val drove a bus for special needs people, and she loved her clients. Each morning she would get NeeNee ready for her center. I would prepare breakfast and then wait for her to make her entrance into the dining room to eat. She always waited for me to tell her how pretty she looked. It makes me laugh when I think about NeeNee's vanity and how she responded when we told her she was pretty.

NeeNee was so small. I always dressed her in little girl clothes. She looked like a little girl. I dressed her pretty, and she wore the best colognes. I felt that she deserved the best that I could give her. She looked pretty, and she smelled sweet. She had natural curly hair that she always messed up after it was combed. No matter how pretty she looked, she would always lie on the floor. I would shake my head and laugh. One thing that the family always laughed about was when there was something on the table that we would tell her not to touch. If she wanted it, she would keep trying until she got it. We would watch as she closed her eyes reaching for the item, thinking that closing her eyes prevented *us* from seeing her. That was a great laugh!

One thing was for sure, though—I could not always laugh at the things NeeNee did. I also shed a lot of very painful tears, but I am very thankful for God's peace that passes all understanding. Whatever the task is that we must do, it is always better when we have a willing mind to work. It was and still is the joy of the Lord that gives me strength.

When we have a job to do, we will do well
when we have a willing mind to work.

Do not sorrow, for the joy of the Lord
is our strength. (Nehemiah 8:10)

Emotions

I carried NeeNee to church, but she didn't enjoy going to church unless she could walk while the service was going on. Although my family understood her actions and our pastor made us feel very welcome, I realized that I could not impose my daughter on other people. Those who are not educated about special needs people sometimes do not know how to respond to them. They miss out on many opportunities to be blessed. NeeNee didn't like to hear the deacons when they prayed long prayers. She tensed up with the loud preaching, but she did like the piano and organ music and the choir singing. She also liked to hear a particular brother in the church sing. NeeNee really loved his singing, and she always reacted with excitement when he would sing. What a blessing his singing was to her. She really loved music. I would take her to choir rehearsal with me sometimes. When my friend Veida, who was our choir director, would stop playing to talk with the choir, NeeNee wanted her to continue playing. She would take her hand and put them on the piano keys to make her start playing again. To see how she related to music always brought joy to the choir members, because they realized that in her own unique way, she could praise the Lord. NeeNee also knew that everything and everyone should praise the Lord.

NeeNee never learned to speak, but she communicated. My daughter's way of communicating was different, but she got her message across. My family and friends have pleasant memories of her unique way of communicating. Her sisters share how she would stomp when they didn't do what she wanted them to do. We named it "the NeeNee stomp." We started mimicking her when she would do it, and that was always fun. One of her sisters remembered how NeeNee would offer comfort when she thought we were upset. She would lay on you with her hand on your face. She would show so much love. She definitely knew what she wanted. NeeNee really loved her sisters. When her oldest sister, Regina, married, she was so jealous that she got angry with her. When Regina would come to the house to visit, NeeNee rejected her affection and would have nothing to do her. Regina actually had to win back her love and affection.

A special blessing, indeed! For twenty years, she laid across me to sleep each night. That's one of her habits that I could not break. Another habit was her ten-o'clock-at-night pudding snack, when she brought her pudding to me with a utensil—a fork, knife, or spoon. She knew you needed to use a utensil in order to feed her. Feeding her was a special time. I would hold my hands out for us to pray together. NeeNee would put her hands in mine so we could bless her food. She understood the routine.

Through the years, I found that repetition was the way she learned. Our talking time was me doing the talking, and sometimes she would get tired of my talking and try to close my mouth. If I sounded sad, she would lay her head on my breast with her hand on my face. That was her way of giving love and comfort.

Each morning when she was dressed, she waited to be told how pretty she was before I fed her breakfast. She wanted to be ready when her bus arrived, and she would get upset when the bus was late. She would lie on the floor and make faces. There was also danger in parenting a special needs person. NeeNee would lay on the floor in front of the furnace, and one day she got so close and her hair caught on fire. Her sisters were terrified when they called me at work. I didn't know what to do, but through that experience I learned to watch her even more. I also prayed that God would bless me financially to be able to replace the wall furnace with central heating. He heard and answered my prayer, although not right away. We had to be extra watchful during the winter months. We watched, but God protected.

I think the best thing that we did for NeeNee was to learn to fit into her world. We must realize that we might be as abnormal to mentally challenged people as we think they are to us. Who is to say what's "normal," because God created us all in His image? We let everyone know that we respected their domain, but when they come to our home, all comfort belonged to Deneen because that was her domain. We felt that she had a right to enjoy life as she knew it, and she did. Imagine how we watched her as she would be at the sofa enjoying her stash. She would move the items around from one place to another. She seemed to get so much enjoyment in what she was doing. If we touched anything, it would really upset her. You see, this was her way of communicating, "I'm enjoying myself!"

The family found out that NeeNee liked one-piece pajamas year-round. When the summer months came, the one-piece pajamas had to be hidden because they were made of flannel and they were too hot. She looked hard in the closet and in the drawers, throwing clothes out. When she could not find them, she would finally settle for the summer outfits. I discovered that she wanted to wear the pajamas at all times one evening after work. When I got home, I found her sitting in the living room holding the pajamas in her arms looking very sad. I had laid out a change of clothes on the bed for her. My friend Bennie, who stayed with her until I got home, did not know that NeeNee didn't like the clothes I left for her to put on. Needless to say, after that communication, it never happened again. My friend said, "You are the dumb one. You should have known."

When NeeNee was visiting with my daughter Karla, my granddaughter Veronica discovered her standing at the top of the stairs. She had taken her clothes off and had somehow located her one-piece pajamas and had them in her hand with her head to one side and a pretty smile.

Veronica said to her mom, "Is NeeNee supposed to be dressed?"

Her mother replied, "Yes, I've dressed her."

However, she discovered NeeNee standing at the top of the stairs undressed, holding her pajamas—totally undressed, but still smiling. NeeNee could not verbalize what she wanted, but she certainly could communicate, and that day Karla got the message! I sincerely believe that Deneen accepted the way God made her, and in her own way, she taught us to also accept His design in our lives because we are all created for God's unique purpose and plan. When we accept who we are, we can sincerely praise Him with all our hearts.

We are all created for God's unique purpose and plan. Let us praise Him with all our hearts.

I will praise you, for I am fearfully and wonderfully made; Marvelous are your works, and that my soul knows very well. (Psalm 139:14)

7

Family

NeeNee was older than all of my grandchildren and nieces and nephews, yet they all surpassed her mentally and physically. That was a heartache I had to overcome, but God gave me the strength to deal with it. When new babies were born into the family, NeeNee always tried to care for them. Sometimes she would even try to pick them up. As I said earlier, she had a way of communicating. When the baby would cry, she would crawl over to the baby with her hand over her eye and lay her head on the baby's stomach. That was her way of caring for the baby. There was the time when NeeNee's nephew, Jason, was playing with her on the floor and accidentally bumped her nose with his elbow. It started to bleed, and we called the paramedics. They rushed NeeNee to the hospital, thinking, along with the emergency room staff, that she had been abused. To hear Jason tell of his love for her and to let it be known that he would never hurt NeeNee in any way filled my heart with pride for the love our family had. She hated that ride in the ambulance! When the doctors saw all of the love around NeeNee, they knew there was no way we would ever mistreat her. The staff had to admit that they could feel the love. She loved it when Jason and Brandon would kiss her and tell her how precious she was.

NeeNee did not like the ambulance rides, but she loved to ride in the car with the music playing. She would sit back and relax, playing with her curly hair. She really enjoyed the music. I loved watching her through the rearview mirror. If a song came on that she did not like, she would grab my hair or pinch me on the shoulder to change the station. A very humorous thing happened with her and her sister Valencia. Valencia was driving, and Deneen wanted the radio station changed. She grabbed Val's ponytail, and it came off. The look on her face as she held the ponytail was unforgettable. Val said, "She really got my attention." That's communication.

My devotional time is almost over, but the day is still full of special memories. I think about the lives of my daughters and how they developed into good mothers. My firstborn, Regina, has one daughter, Brandi; my second daughter, Valencia, has three sons, Daymein, Jason, and Brandon.

My third daughter, Karla, has a son and daughter, Grant and Veronica. My third daughter gave me a son through marriage—picked out by NeeNee—and what a choice she made. NeeNee truly loved her brother-in-law. He was so great with her and also a loving son to me. She had a special language that she spoke only to him.

Even my grandchildren and great-grandchildren knew that their aunt was special. As I taught their mothers, their mothers also taught them to love their aunt, as well as all people with special needs. The doctor told me that she would do much better in a family that loved her. He was so right, because we truly loved her.

We found out early in her life that NeeNee didn't like change. When I would try new foods, she had a way of letting me know she didn't like them. She liked certain foods, and that was that! She would stop eating if I tried to give her something new. We all knew everything had to stay in its place. I could not rearrange the furniture without displeasing her. If I moved a vase from one table to another, I subsequently would see that vase back where I moved it from. At first I thought one of the other girls had done it, but after talking with them, we realized who was replacing things. If you moved a picture from one wall to another, that just wouldn't work with NeeNee. She would take my hand and raise it toward the picture, and after a while, I knew she wanted me to change it. Since she couldn't reach the picture, I could leave it there, and finally she would forget about. I communicated no! She accepted it.

If we moved anything out of place, she worried us and worried us until it was put back. Then she would push us away. I remember the time when I was sitting in the living room, and I heard this noise in the hall—the sound of someone struggling. When I investigated the noise in the hall, there was NeeNee trying to carry a large potted plant back into the living room where I had moved it from. She was so serious! She didn't want the plant in the den, where I thought it looked good. The fight was on, but she won! When I tried to put the plant back in the den, she grabbed my hand, and she communicated no! I smile as I can still see this very small person trying to move a very large plant. We don't understand why God chooses certain people for certain tasks, but if we trust Him, He will bring us through with victory. That is another assurance through His word.

We must trust God in all situations of
life with assurance of victory.

And we know that all things work together for
good to those who love God, to those who are the
called according to His purpose. (Romans 8:28)

I realize that everyone who is blessed with special needs children may not feel as I do. I find nothing wrong with that. People must deal with their situations in their own ways. There is no way I would pass judgment on a parent who is unable to keep his or her child. Knowing that NeeNee was my child and that God had blessed me as His means of transportation to bring her to earth for a little while, I am very happy that He knew I would be able to handle the task He had for me to do. God gave me strength that I didn't even know I had.

I've had people say, "Ann, I don't know how you did it. I don't think I could have kept a child in that condition."

My answer was always the same: "If that's what God called you to do, then you would have been able to do it."

Did I get tired? Yes! Did I become discouraged? Yes! Did I get angry? Yes! Did I feel pain when other mothers had healthy children? Yes! Did I want to hear her say, "Mommy"? Yes! Did I want to hear her say, "I love you"? Yes! She never called me Mommy, but she knew I was her mother. She never said, "I love you," but I know she loved me. But through it all—the anger and the pain—I have no regrets. I would do it again and again, because I miss her so very much. He knows exactly what He's doing. And He carried me through the tiredness, the discouragement, the anger, and the pain. Yes, my heavenly Father carried me through it all. God is faithful to His promise. Speaking of anger, I remember the time NeeNee received a letter from the Social Help Agency stating that she was now able to go to work. She was about twenty-five years old. I was to bring her into the office to discuss employment. I made an appointment with them. I dressed her as pretty as I could and put on her sweet-smelling cologne, and off we went. It angered me because I realized they paid no attention to a person's file. The clients are just numbers, not people. When we arrived, there were strange stares from the people in the waiting area and also the attending agent and other employees.

The agent who helped me was in a state of shock when he saw NeeNee. When she started to make her playing noise, I thought he was going to pass out. Then there were the trips to the copy machine from the other people in the office. They wanted to see where the strange sound was coming from. Needless to say, to the embarrassment of the agent, there were no jobs found that met with her qualifications. Although I realize that they work with many people, it would be wonderful if the people in these positions would at least read about the histories of the people that they are serving. It would be wonderful if they could realize that the clients are human beings and not file numbers. They would get to know some very special people. Being angry and hurt sometimes is part of the task. Even in this, God gives us the strength.

8

Friends

The memories are joyful but painful on this day of my reflections about a special child who was a special blessing to my family. I decided throughout the day to ask some of my friends to tell me of a special memory they had about NeeNee. I smiled when one of my friends told me the things she remembered. NeeNee loved clothes. The way she acted when she was dressed pretty was memorable. Yes, she did love to look pretty. She would not let one my friends touch her tennis shoes. She was very selfish about her belongings. She was always happy when people came to visit. She would always offer them a seat. She would take their hands, lead them to a chair, and almost push them down in the chair.

One of my friends told me that she remembered how NeeNee would close the door when they were visiting in the summer. We had the door opened to keep cool from the heat. Sometimes when my friends were over, she would lie on the sofa to keep them from sitting down. When she got tired of company, she would get their purses and coats. One of my friends who would come over always spoke very softly to her. NeeNee always wanted her to stay for a long visit. One of my dear friends, Jessie, was always the one I called on during those emergency trips to the hospital. She would come over to visit, and we found that NeeNee had a sense of humor. She would always get in front of Jessie and make a very sad face. Jessie would say, "NeeNee, don't do that!" After NeeNee did it, she would smile. I told Jessie that she was the only person NeeNee would do that to. That was NeeNee's way of having a special rapport with Jessie. Maybe NeeNee remembered that Jessie was with us on many of those trips to emergency room with us. Who's to say?

Although NeeNee never spoke, she always knew each person who came to visit. She could be quite the hostess when she wanted to be. She was very strong, although she only weighed ninety-eight pounds and was only four foot ten. NeeNee had traveled a long way since birth. Fifty years ago, it was a very strange thing that the psychiatrists and psychologists, although they dealt with mental health issues, could not understand the progress of a mentally challenged child. When I carried NeeNee to her doctor visits and told them of her progress, they would always ask me the same question: "Is she speaking yet?" If the child could not verbalize words, they didn't accept what they did as progress. That was very discouraging to me as a mother because they didn't realize that these children still have many ways of communicating, and my NeeNee was really a great communicator! I am happy that things have changed since her birth. The medical profession now realizes that there are no limits to what God can do with

His special creations. She continued to progress as God would have her progress.

NeeNee brought love to all who knew her. I remember the time my brother Eddie was visiting us from Fort Worth, Texas, and she showed him so much love. He went to visit with my oldest daughter, Regina, for a few days. When Regina brought him back to my home, NeeNee went to the door, and she grabbed his arm to pull him inside. Then she pushed her sister out of the door and closed it. It was her way of letting her uncle know that she was happy he was back. The way she reacted to her uncle brought joy to his heart. As I said before, special people like NeeNee have so much love to give. All we have to do is receive it with open arms and open hearts.

After my other daughters were no longer living at home, NeeNee and I were alone for fifteen years. Those years were so special. I would get her off to the center each morning and then go to work. After her time at the center, she would stay with my friend Doris until I got home from work. It was a comfort to know she was also happy until I was there to get her. We had special time together. If I were on the phone too long, she would pull at the phone. She wanted all of my attention. Even if I were on the telephone or the computer, she would come to me with a hug to get all of my attention. If I got involved in a television show, she would stand in front of the TV pretending to be interested. If I would ask her to move, she would wring her hands and look at me. My time was supposed to be for her. I wanted to know where she was also, or else I could face a flooded kitchen or sit in a dark house. But most of the time, I would find her really enjoying herself with her stash. When bedtime came, as I mentioned earlier, she refused to sleep in her own bedroom. She was only comfortable sleeping across me. I miss that, although I complained when she was doing it. I miss that special bond that we had.

Happy Forever

As I sit here, I smile. I remember the two poems God blessed me to write and decide to read them. As I read them, it makes me reflect on just how happy NeeNee made me. The first poem I was inspired to write is called "Our Special Blessing." I received so much joy when I wrote that poem. I expressed exactly what was in my heart. That was the way I saw my daughter and the task that was given to me. When we accept the will of God for our lives, knowing that He is the one in charge, it is true poetry. We are told in Ecclesiastes 3:11, "God has made everything beautiful in its time." Every special needs person is a creation of God's beauty. The second poem I wrote is called "God Created Special People." I wrote it after realizing just how far God had brought NeeNee. I am so greatly blessed to have been chosen to be her mother, because she taught me how to truly love unconditionally.

Through writing these poems, I let it be known that God is still good and makes no mistakes. I also realized that with her, I did not have an ordinary life. My life was filled with the wonderment of the Lord, proving to me that with Him all things are possible, for the Lord is great and greatly to be praised. As I read them now, I feel the warmth of God's love as I remember the power of His blessings. In writing these poems, I had told myself that they would be published one day, for all people to know that my NeeNee and other special needs people are very special indeed. As I read the poems, I also think about two other people who are special to me. One is Bertha, a thirty-six-year-old who has Down syndrome. No one can say, "I love you, Ann Grant," like she can. The other person is Samantha, who is twelve years old and has cerebral palsy. There is always a loving smile on her face, and she calls me "Auntie Ann." Both of them are blessed to be with their mothers, who accepted the task God called them to do. There is so much love communicated through their lives.

Through it all it is the Lord's
faithfulness that has kept me.

It is good that one should hope and wait quietly for
the salvation of the Lord. (Lamentations 3:26)

It is time for me to get up and go to the kitchen, but I sit back down. I begin laughing about all of the things that were unique in NeeNee's life. I am thinking about how she didn't let people sit on the sofa unless she wanted them there. I remember the times we would have company, and NeeNee stretched out on the sofa to keep the people from sitting there. After our company left, she started putting her things back on the sofa with an attitude. That was my Missy, as I sometimes called her. I think about how she enjoyed going to her center every day to be with her special needs friends and how she loved riding the bus. I think about the items in her stash on the sofa that made her happy. Some were the oddest things, but these are the things that made her happy.

Of course, most of the things belonged to other people she claimed as her own. Once she possessed them, they were hers. Most of the time the family would not fight with her over these things. As long as she was happy, we were happy. I laugh aloud as I recollect looking for things that were missing. We would just look on the sofa and the item was usually there, but we would have to sneak the things away. If she saw us, she would express her displeasure. As mentioned, NeeNee's stash consisted of all of the items that were special to her. Her sister Karla brought her some pink beads from Hawaii. She did not allow anyone to touch them. She let you know that those beads belonged to her, and they were off limits to anyone else. If you attempted to touch them, she would sling those beads so hard that they would hit you as she put them behind her back and pushed you away. Complete ownership!

Her musical stuffed animals were also off limits to

everyone unless she wanted to show them to you. She would snatch them out of your hand and place them back on the sofa, unless she wanted you to wind the musical ones so she could hear them sing. Her favorite one was a lion that Valencia bought her. It sang, "You Are So Beautiful to Me." After you would wind it up for her, she would take it back and enjoy the song. Yes, my life with Missy was quite a life. I look from the kitchen into the living room at the sofa, where some of her stash remains. The items remain there because one young woman said to me, "You should keep some of NeeNee's things on your sofa because they meant so much to her." I realized what she said was true, which is the reason I still keep a portion of NeeNee's stash on my sofa.

10

If You Could See Me Now

I think about NeeNee's final days in the hospital. I really believed I would be bringing her home. But during that final Wednesday at about 4:00 a.m., she woke up and reached her hands up toward heaven. I thought she needed an embrace from her mother, so I hugged her tightly and laid her back down, but I did not realize she was telling me she loved me and was saying goodbye. When I woke up after drifting back off to sleep, I kissed her and called her name and embraced her, but there was no response. I cried out to the nurse. She came and checked Deneen and got no response. Then the nurse called code blue. The medical staff tried to revive her, but there was still no response. NeeNee was now home with God. I found it hard to believe as the staff said to me, "We are so sorry." I cannot explain the pain I felt. As my family came into the room, I found joy from my daughter Karla, and her words brought comfort to my heart in that painful moment when she looked at her baby sister and said, "Oh, NeeNee, the first words you ever spoke were to Jesus our Lord."

The pain of loss will always be with me, but through the pain, God still gives me His peace and joy. I truly miss being with her and receiving her special kind of love, but God knows best, and everything works in His timing—not ours.

I find joy in knowing that Deneen was *our special blessing* that we had for only a short while. But if she could she would say to us, "If you could only see me now." She is with Jesus, and she is whole and walking straight. She is perfect in every way. Although she did not like change when she was with me, this change into eternity is not bothering her at all. She is happily praising the Lord with words that she could not utter when she was here—with those little fat hands raised in adoration to God. I truly thank God for *Deneen—our special blessing!*

And God will wipe away every tear from their
eyes; and there shall be no more death, nor sorrow,
nor crying. There shall be no more pain, for the
former things have passed away. (Revelation 21:4)

I am so grateful that I was blessed to be the mother
of someone so very special—a gift of love that only God
can give. The precious memories of my baby Deneen
will always be with me. I will always ponder over those
memories of her life as I hold them in my heart. I can
truly say that our God knows exactly who to assign each
task in life to.

The task is over, but there is still work to be done,
because God always has something for His people to do. I
am still willing to be used by God to be a blessing in any
way that will bring glory to His name. What a blessing it
is to know that God will use us to be a blessing in the lives
of others.

And the King will answer and say to them, assuredly, I say to you, inasmuch as you did it to one of the least of these my brethren, you did it to me. (Matthew 25:40)

Our Family's Blessing

Ann P. Grant, October 1980

"What a pretty baby," is what was always said,
But there were unanswered questions
That I pondered in my head.

Lord, something is wrong, and I can plainly see
She's not responding like her sisters, did it seem to me.
"What is it, Lord?" was the question I would ask.
He answered and said, "I have for you a
Very special task."

He said, "A special blessing I have just for you
Because it's a task that only you can do.
I know it will be hard, and you do really understand,
But you will not be alone. I will always walk with
you and hold your hand.

"This is a perfect gift for your family,
Just you wait and see.
She's a special blessing created for you by Me.
I know with this blessing you will have terrible pain,
But continue to love her and be happy because
You have a great reward to gain.

"Her look will be different and straight.
She will never walk.
You will never hear her say "Mom," "Mama," or
"Mother," because she will never talk.
But she will have love that's truly from her heart,
Special love that I will give her from the very start.

"You will not be alone with her, because
her sisters will be there too,
Giving their love and support, and together
you will make it through.

"Family and friends will give encouraging words
to help along the way,
But most of all My presence will be with you
as you talk with Me each day.

"I make no mistakes in all the way I lead.
There will be blessings for your family
with each loving deed.
Her sisters will work to make her happy
And enjoy the funny things she will do.
Her way of communicating will get through to you.

"You will teach your family through example
To look up and not down,
To trust God with a smile and never wear a frown.
Do not be ashamed of her but shower
Her with love
Because she's your special blessing sent
From God above."

Our Blessing Is Home

January 15, 2009

The task is over now.
Our special blessing is with the Lord.
In our lives, there is pain and sorrow
and a very great void.
We truly know we will see her again
When Jesus takes us all home, where joy will never end.

All right, Ann, your devotional time for today is over. Your time with the Lord was so fulfilling. You have also been blessed with the time you spent with your memories, but those pies cannot make themselves. It's best you get busy!